ISBN 978-1-333-39158-4
PIBN 10496886

1 MONTH OF
FREE
READING

at

www.ForgottenBooks.com

By purchasing this book you are eligible for one month membership to ForgottenBooks.com, giving you unlimited access to our entire collection of over 1,000,000 titles via our web site and mobile apps.

To claim your free month visit:

www.forgottenbooks.com/free496886

THE VILLAGE COMMUNITY

AND

MODERN PROGRESS.

BY

ANANDA K. COOMARASWAMY.

REPRINTED FROM
THE CEYLON NATIONAL REVIEW,
VOL. II. No. 7.

PRINTED BY
THE COLOMBO APOTHECARIES CO., LTD.,
1908.

CARPENTIER

THE VILLAGE COMMUNITY

AND

MODERN PROGRESS.*

THE choice of this subject depends upon the fact that within the organization of the village community we find developed so many of the essentials of a true nationality. I allude particularly to economic security in the broadest sense, and to the evolution of personal character and a capacity for concerted action.

In speaking of economic security, I refer to the position of the Sinhalese villager, contrasted with that of a wage labourer in one of the large towns of modern India or Ceylon, or upon a tea estate. The essential feature of the land system of the last two or three thousand years has been an inseparable association between each man and a part of the land which descended in his family from generation to generation. This land was not his own property in the sense that he could easily sell it, but his tenancy was secure so long as he performed the services, due in respect of it, to king, chieftain, or temple. Society was founded upon the direct relation of mankind to the soil from which rice, the staple food, was directly obtained. To every man in this society a place was automatically assigned by a legal and religious sanction, and the exercise of his particular function was at once his duty and his pride.

More than one Government official has noted from time to time the disastrous results of the decay of the organized society of the villages. Speaking of Sabaragamuwa, in a report† written nearly ninety years ago, Mr. Turnour traced the then existing agricultural depression to the weakening of the power of the proprietors through the substitution of the grain tax for all other dues and taxes, the result of which measure was that tenants "ceased to render dues or labour to the proprietor."

* Presidential Address to the Ceylon Social Reform Society, May, 1908.
† Service Tenures Commission, 1872, p. 466.

The chiefs then, says Mr. Turnour, "possessing no authority....were unable to command labour on any terms, and, reduced as they were in their circumstances, they could not afford to pay the hire, if money was to procure it for them....If the present separation between proprietor and dependent is made permanent, landed property becomes at once disconnected and divided into many little separated estates.....:Neither can capital be created or industry excited by sudden impulses. A community of interests must in the present state of the Colony be the foundation upon which individual wealth is raised....The tenure by which lands were formerly held happily combined these objects." The most important part of this statement is the stress laid upon the necessity for *community of interest.*

The commutation of services has also weakened the basis of Sinhalese society;[*] it has indeed struck at the root of the personal relation between proprietor and tenant, replacing it by a pecuniary relation. The power[†] of tenants to alienate service lands has had the same effect.[‡] Not a few Agents of Government have doubted the desirability of these interferences with the structure of the Sinhalese village. Mr. Russell, Government Agent of the Central Province, says[§] in a statement showing his appreciation of the importance of village solidarity:

"In my Administration Report for 1870 I mentioned that neither the actual condition of service tenants nor the relations between them and their landlords rendered necessary the abolition of Service Tenures in the Central Province. Since that Report was written, the Gansabhawa Ordinance, No. 26 of 1871, has been passed. The object of this Ordinance is, by the *restoration of communal self-government,* to enable the *inhabitants of every village to manage their own purely local affairs* in respect of the execution and maintenance of village paths, ambalamas, etc., provision of education of children, for breeding of cattle, preservation of pasturage, and other common purposes, and also in respect of the decision of trifling civil actions and petty criminal complaints. Now, the destruction of the influence of the natural leaders of the people, which must be the inevitable result, if it were not the object, of the Service Tenures Ordinance, may, without hesitation, be asserted to be quite incompatible with the ends which the Gansabhawa Ordinance

[*] Service Tenures Commission, 1872, p. 459.
[†] " Practically a creation of our own Courts," J. F. Dickson, Service Tenures Commission, 1872.
[‡] I am not now arguing for any attempt at the restoration of the village system in the exact form it formerly possessed, but I seek merely to demonstrate the disadvantages resulting from the absence of any such system, and of the replacement of community of interest, by diversity of interest amongst the people of a village; and to suggest the importance of conserving and strengthening what remains of the common life of the villages.
[§] Service Tenures Commission Report, 1872, p. 456.   Italics are mine.

seeks to obtain. Believing therefore, that *the institution of Village Councils contains the elements of great material and moral progress for the Kandyans*, I cannot but view the commutation of services as a grave political mistake." It may be that, as in Europe, the commutation of services has been a social change, the progress of which it would have been impossible to resist or reverse ; but if so, the point that I wish to emphasize is that of endeavouring to preserve or restore in some way, not necessarily the same way, the community of interest, and capacity for concerted action for a common end which were so characteristic of the old system ; for if this cannot be done, we shall have to confess that the " progress " of the nineteenth century has availed us little.

The value and importance of the existing remains of village community organization cannot be better illustrated than in the following extract from a Report by Mr. Dickson, regarding the district of Nuwara-kalawiya and contrasting it in this respect with other Provinces.

"The point in which the political condition of this Province especially differs from that of the rest of Ceylon is, that here the original Oriental village still remains of a pure and simple type, while in the rest of Ceylon it has generally disappeared under the influence of Foreign Government and the jurisdiction of English Courts....the villages....have retained, almost in its pristine purity, the ancient village system of the Aryan races. The discovery of this political state of the new Province at once suggested the necessity for the greatest care in avoiding any measures which would suddenly break up this system. To this end, and to utilise the existing system, it was decided to introduce throughout the Province the Village Communities Ordinance, which, though passed by the Legislature in ignorance of the existence of the perfect ' villages' of Nuwarakalawiya, is admirably adapted to their organization. It is to the extent to which this excellent Ordinance, No. 26 of 1871, has been adopted, and the success which has attended its working, that is to be attributed the essential difference in the system pursued in this Province, as distinguished from the six older Provinces, and the *marked extent to which the people themselves have contributed to the general improvement of the country*. In the other Provinces if anything has to be done, down comes the tax gatherer : everything has to be paid for. Here the people give their labour gratuitously for common objects, and escape all special taxation. In the other Provinces police are required, and are paid for by a special tax. Here there are no police....

"Here the irrigation works, except so far as the Government assists, are restored by the united unpaid labour of the landowners. In the other Provinces, except in the few cases and to the limited extent that the system of this Province has been adopted, all improvements in irrigation have to be paid for by money contributions from the landowners, recovered with great difficulty and often opposition. In the other Provinces tolls are imposed even on the minor roads. Here the people make their own roads* with their unpaid labour, and remain free from tolls."

One cannot but wish that all Government servants, that is, our servants, had approached the matter in a similar spirit. Take, for example, the village rights to the produce of neighbouring jungles. These have never been well defined, but certainly the villagers have always been accustomed to be able to obtain wood for building and agricultural purposes, firewood, jungle ropes, medicines, dyeing plants, honey and wax and such things from the forests. The endeavour of Government seems to have been, however, not to contribute to the villagers' prosperity and security in such matters, but to restrict their rights as much as possible, generally on the plea of forest conservation, and with much condemnation of the harm done by chena cutting. Personally I find it most difficult to distinguish between the harm so done, and the harm done by the sale of lands for tea or rubber estates to such an extent that, as in some parts of the Matale district, whole villages have been destroyed as the result of the continual encroachment upon the free area about them. Again, instead of forest regulation being communal, or even in the hands of the local Agent of Government, it is in the hands of a centralised Forest Department whose main object is to run the forests as a business concern, and whose hope is to get credit for a larger revenue; and the result is that we get the great Department suing a poor woman for stealing five cents worth of firewood (*Times of Ceylon*, 1/9/03). These are small matters perhaps, but show which way the wind blows. A Government official once said to me that it would be as much as a Government Agent's place was worth to refuse a villager the right to cut timber for agricultural purposes—say making a plough; I accepted the statement. Subsequently I found that when, acting myself for Government, I required a little timber for use for Government purposes, it was considered perfectly useless to apply for it to the Forest Department, owing to the extent of the formalities to be gone through in the various circumlocution offices, and the only way was to buy it in the market. I then understood why the villager was able to say that he could no longer get wood for his plough or jungle ropes for his *ankeliya*. Sometimes too, the *ampitiya*, or plain where *ankeliya* was played, is now Government or private property.

I propose now to say a few words about the personal character of the real and unspoilt Sinhalese villager; and the evidence on this

* Such communal roads, made by the adult male inhabitants, are called *pinparaval*, 'paths of merit' (Manual North Central Province, p. 207).

point is so strong, that it cannot be overlooked. If therefore it can now be shown that violence or crime are to any marked degree prevalent in the villages, it would appear that this must be due to some flaw in the "civilising" influences brought to bear upon them in one way or another during the last century. Such flaws it would be but too easy to indicate; they include the growth of an opium and liquor traffic, the encouragement of litigation, education which ignores the traditional religion and established sanctions for morality, and lastly, but perhaps not least important, destruction of the established order of society and decay of the hereditary peasant proprietor.

I give now some quotations that witness to the character of the true Sinhalese villager. Speaking of one of the most isolated and typically "village-community" districts fifty years ago, Mr. A. O. Brodie* wrote: "The people of Nuwarakalawiya are the most gentle I have had the good fortune to meet...Serious assaults, robberies, murders, are all but unknown, and during three years I have not had to punish one native of the district for pilfering." Davy,† ninety years ago, remarked: "Among few people are family attachments more strong and sincere; there is little to divert or weaken them; and they are strengthened equally by their mode of life and their religion." A piece of evidence more often quoted is taken from a report made by Mr. Lushington in 1870: "There is annually a gathering from all parts of the Island at Anuradhapura to visit what are called sacred places. I suppose about 20,000 people come here, remain for a few days, and then leave. There are no houses for their reception, but under the grand umbrageous trees of our park-like environs they erect their little booths and picnic in the open air. As the height of the festival approaches, the place becomes instinct with life; and when there is no room left to camp in, the later comers unceremoniously take possession of the verandahs of the public buildings. So orderly is their conduct, however, that no one thinks of disturbing them. The old Kacceri stands, a detached building not far from the bazaar, and about one-eighth of a mile from the Assistant Agent's house. Till lately the treasure used to be lodged in a little iron box that a few men could easily run away with, guarded by three native treasury watchers. There lay this sum of money, year after year, at the mercy of any six men who chose to run with it into the neighbouring jungle—once in, detection was almost impossible—and yet no one ever supposed the attempt would be made. These 20,000 people from all parts of the country come and go annually without a single policeman being here; and, as the Magistrate of the district, I can only say that anything to surpass their

* J. C. B. R. A. S., Vol. III., p. 161.
† Travels in Ceylon, p. 289.

decorum and sobriety of conduct it is impossible to conceive. Such a thing as a row is unheard of. That does not look like a people among whom crime of a heinous nature was indigenous! In what part of Christendom would the money box be safe?" The testimony of Bennett* to the character of the inhabitants of another district, the Magampattu, may also be quoted: "I had heard so much to the prejudice of the inhabitants, before an opportunity offered of judging how far reports were, or were not, correct, that the first thing I did, upon taking charge of the district, was to erect a flogging post in the bazaar. This naturally gave rise to the supposition, that they had *a terrible Tartar* come amongst them; but after an experience of twelve months as the only Magistrate in the district, during which period I had neither occasion to commit one native for trial, or to resort to summary punishment within my own jurisdiction, (extending over seventy-six miles in length), either by the lash or imprisonment, except in one instance of the latter, in order to give a place of refuge to a Malabar vagrant, I had the supreme pleasure of ordering the removal of the *maiden* flogging post, as the last act of my authority there: and, when the extent of the district is considered, this tribute is nothing more than is, in justice, due to the native inhabitants of the Mahagampattoo, whom I left, *malgré* all that I had suffered there, with heartfelt regret."

Perhaps however the most important testimony to the character of the Kandyan villager, and the value of the common culture of which he was a part, is given by Knox: "Their ordinary *Plowmen* and *Husbandmen*" he says, "do speak elegantly, and are full of compliment. And there is no difference between the ability and speech of a Countryman and a Courtier." There was a Sinhalese proverb, to this effect: Take a ploughman from the plough and wash off his dirt, and he is fit to rule a kingdom. "This was spoken," says Knox, "of the people of Cande Uda .... because of the Civility, Understanding and Gravity of the poorest men among them." It would, I suppose, be hard to give stronger proof of the value of a social system capable of producing such results. This was indeed the "spiritual feudalism whereby caste makes a peasant in all his poverty one of the aristocrats of humanity."

We may or may not desire to transcend the idea and the ideal of caste or aristocracy; we may or may not regret the decay of the old and simple agricultural society; but if we are devoted to the future welfare of our own people, we must at least ask of the future that it shall be satisfied with no less a standard than the past attained. That standard involved the binding together of all men, independently of rank and wealth, by means of a common culture.

* Ceylon and its Capabilities, London, 1843, p. 304.

"By their fruits ye shall judge them;" and, judged by this test, who shall say that the new order has improved upon the old? If ever it is to do so, we ourselves must see to it; for the millenium will not steal upon us as a thief in the night.

In most countries these problems attract at least some attention and their importance is to some degree recognised; in one or two of the smallest countries they have been partly solved, as we shall see; but *we* seem to think that if only we drift gently and quietly enough with the current, all these good fishes will swim into our mouths unsought.

It is true that we have not the advantage and stimulus of free political institutions on the one hand, nor of the manifested ideal of kingly government on the other.

We have not the advantage of a ruler like the Gaekwar of Baroda, we have not a ruler who is one of ourselves and understands the ideals of our civilisation. The Gaekwar of Baroda has, (in Mr. Nevinson's words) "restored the ancient village Panchayat, or local government, by the men whom villagers can trust, whereas, in our passion for rigid and centralised power, we have almost destroyed the last vestige of this national training for self-government." That is the essence of what I am trying to say; local government and the capacity for concerted action in communal affairs are the best training for self-government. But all present social tendencies are destructive, not constructive in this respect. We have with us already developed to some degree the "town and country" problem of Europe. The country is becoming less interesting, and affords less scope for the exercise of educated faculties. The sons of country families are not interested in agriculture, but seek to become lawyers, doctors, etc., and especially to be employed under Government. There is no longer vigorous life and common interests to hold together the different village elements—proprietor and tenant, priest and chieftain. For this we have to blame, as I have suggested, in part, a mistaken political action; but in as great or in a greater degree, social causes which are largely under our own control.

What then can we do? It is not easy in a few words to make suggestions regarding so difficult a problem; for it is here as always, not so much in schemes and methods that salvation lies, as in a change of heart; we have not so much to win a victory over others as over ourselves. We have to restore social unity to the ideal of our national life. We must recreate that community of interest between men of different classes, in which lay the strength of the old society, without returning to the limited outlook that has become its weakness.

There is perhaps no country which has more satisfactorily solved the questions we are now considering, than Denmark. The general form of land tenure is now peasant proprietorship; a century ago it was in a general way feudal.   The same change has been, as we have seen, taking place in Ceylon ; but whereas the result has been here disintegration, in Denmark there has been continuous constructive progress. Denmark, an essentially agricultural country, is one of the richest in the world in proportion to its population.   In more important ways the people are also well advanced ; for example, public houses are practically unknown in the country ; farmers, and even small peasants nearly always have a small library of the standard works by Scandinavian authors.   "Each village has its own Parish Council, which levies a Parish rate for its own purposes ; and every village is kept in a clean and sanitary condition.   Generally a hall has been erected by the villages, where during the evenings gymnastics are freely indulged in by the young men of the village.   Some evenings are devoted to dancing, and on Sunday afternoon some person comes over to the village, and either gives a lecture on a historical or topical subject, or a leading man in the village will institute a debate upon some subject of practical value. These lectures and debates are most eagerly attended by all the people in the neighbourhood. .... No poverty apparently exists in the country."

The Danes themselves explain their prosperity as the result of the system of National Education.   All children in Denmark are obliged to attend the National Schools until the age of fourteen.   The chief point to be noticed about these schools is that the foundation of all tuition is religion, and national history.   (You will observe that these are *the* two subjects ignored in most Ceylon schools).   From the National Schools, a majority of young people pass to the Continuation Schools and thence to the Popular High Schools and Agricultural Colleges.   It is worth while to repeat that the Danes attribute their prosperity in a very large degree to the character of the National Education, for we shall find that the aims and methods of this education are as different from the aims and methods of education in Ceylon as light from darkness.   The aims of the schools are: " First and foremost to foster the love of country and national feeling. . . . The second aim is to educate the people that they may make full use of their free constitution ; and the third, to prepare the young to better fit them for the fight for existence, which is daily becoming more acute.   To attain these objects the first essential appears to be to develope the personal character and to make the young man and woman true and honest Danes.   To do this, they rely more on lectures, giving instructive and interesting examples of the history and teaching the best of the literature of the nation, than anything else. . . . The same ideas with regard to education prevail throughout the Agricultural Colleges, national character and history being more important than anything else, concurrently with the development of which, courses in agricultural instruction are given. . . . The courses of instruction consist of National History and Literature (which in all cases stands out foremost), Physics, Chemistry, Natural History, Anatomy, Physiology, with practical demonstrations.

"Education does not end with leaving school or College. A students' club, established in 1882, adopted as its motto: ' Association with the other classes of the population,' and undertakes the organisation of meetings, to which persons of all political and religious views are invited, with the object of creating a more complete understanding and fostering a more liberal public spirit among all classes and sections of the people. Evening lessons for the working classes have been a marked success. Over 100 teachers, chiefly male and female students of the University of Copenhagen, without any pay, every week during the winter months give lectures and demonstrations in different parts of the country to working men and women. . . . To render this instruction for the working classes more successful, cheap text books, written in simple language and sold at nominal prices, have been published. . . . A Committee has been formed at Copenhagen whose members accompany rural excursions to the public buildings and museums in the city, and give the fullest instruction on all objects of interest free of charge. Owing to the existence of this Committee, hundreds of rural excursions are organized every year to visit the museum, picture galleries and antiquarian collections, and with the happiest results. . . .

"A free theatre was brought into existence in 1891, in order that the rural population might be afforded the opportunity of witnessing the best plays of Danish and Norwegian authors at intervals. . . . Moreover, a series of concerts is held throughout the year, to which work-people and peasants are admitted at a nominal charge, and thus every element instrumental in the creation of a vigorous and happy national life is brought into frequent contact with even the humblest stratum of society.

"These various societies, organized and maintained by university men in all parts of Denmark, bring the academical world into close relationship with all classes in the country, and establish a sort of universal national union of vast influence in the material, social, and intellectual progress of the country.

"The problem presented to educationalists in Denmark was: 'How to impart a certain amount of intellectual culture to the people without putting them out of conceit with agricultural work.' The solution was found in the Popular High Schools, and almost every educated Dane will at once assert that the great economic results achieved by the Danish people are in a great measure due to these establishments. . . . the Danish Popular system of education, and the thousand and one forms of organisation that have sprung from it, have rendered Denmark absolutely free of the existence of what might be described as a lower order, or one without well-defined vital interest and standing apart from the spiritual life of the nation. . . .

"The result of this patriotic and practical system of peasant education unquestionably justifies the high compliment paid to the Danish peasantry by the Norwegian poet, Bjornson, who describes them as 'the best enlightened peasantry in the world.' . . . The highest in the land are proud to associate with the humblest artisan and farm labourer in the consciousness that the outcome of such association will be to strengthen the intellectual energies of the nation and elevate the wealth-producer's conception of the duties and responsibilities of citizenship."

I make no apology for quoting thus largely from a Report on Co-operative Agriculture and Rural Conditions in Denmark, published by the Department of Agriculture and Technical Instruction for Ireland, for this system of education, under conditions not unlike our own, has produced in the people of Denmark, a common culture and intelligence, which can fairly be compared with that attributed by Knox to the Kandyan people in the seventeenth century, and which it would seem so difficult to restore under the altered conditions now obtaining here. But what has been done in Denmark can be done here, if the will is ours; we also can restore a common culture and community of interest between all classes and all districts, and something of the old capacity for concerted action. But this cannot be done without labour and sacrifice, of the inconspicuous kind. We are not likely in the immediate future to possess the stimulus of free political institutions; but I think the roots of nationality lie deeper than the outward forms of government, in the national culture and traditions, and it is possible for us to work at the restoration of these in ways which have but little connection with the administration of Government. Perhaps the first step to be taken is to press more and more for a local University, and to make no pretence that we do not want, in doing so, to nationalize education in Ceylon. For our real aim must be to educate the people (not a special class alone) through the medium of their own national culture, exactly as is done in Denmark.

In the meantime there is much that can be done with existing opportunities. Suppose, for example, we should start a students' club in Colombo, adopting as its motto: " Association with all classes of the population" and that from this club should be sent out lecturers and speakers on Sinhalese history and literature and kindred subjects, on Indian history, the relation of Ceylon to India, and, in co-operation with the Agricultural Society, on all sorts of agricultural subjects. We should get agricultural progress much quicker by thus giving to it as in Denmark, a vital national interest, than by making the Agricultural Society practically a Government Department as at present.

An institution we might with advantage adopt, is called in England the "Summer School;" such schools might be held annually at Anuradhapura in the pilgrim season. For a period of six weeks a series of lectures on subjects of national interest might be given by our best informed and most enthusiastic workers; think how interested the intelligent villager would be (and if not, my own experience of him has been misleading) in enthusiastic lectures on the history and significance of the Village Community in Ceylon and other countries, combined with an account of some of the many suggestions that have been made by social reformers in all countries with regard to the restoration of the advantages of the village system; how this would enable him better and more loyally to work with his own Gansabhawa. How interested and educated also he would be by lectures on the history of Buddhism, with lantern pictures, not only of Anuradhapura, but of the other great Buddhist remains in India and Java, or in an address on Buddhist art in the East generally.

It is not indeed by teaching him about the Norman Conquest or the Geography of France that his outlook will be widened and his intelligence developed; it is by enabling him to grasp more firmly and deeply the principles underlying some of the things of which he already knows a little, and in which his interest is already awakened, that he will be enabled to progress, and that public spirit and the capacity for co-operation will be re-awakened in him, with the growing sense of nationality and individuality in his people and himself.

Another institution that has lately come much to the front in England is the historical pageant. Suppose such a pageant were held every few years in Anuradhapura. It might be made an object lesson in history and civic ideals. What magnificent and inspiring scenes could be revived before us, and how easily; for the people themselves would understand and become their own teachers once the idea began to take a hold upon them. The conversation between Mahinda and Devanampiyatissa, Dutṭha Gamanii planning the Ruvanveli Dāgaba; Elāva; Gaja Bāhu; the coming of the Tooth-relic; Buddhadāsa; Fa Hien; Parākrama Bāhu the Great; the marriage of Padmāvati; Toṭagamuva; the arrival of the Portuguese and of the Dutch; Kīrti Srī Rāja Siṇha and his brothers, who were "one with the religion and the people;" the Saṇgha Rāja; the last King of Kandy:—what an education the representation of such scenes by the people and for the people could be.

But more important even than all these means and methods, more important, if possible, than the nationalisation of education, is the cultivation of faithfulness and unity amongst ourselves. Of what avail is it to know that Municipal institutions are not an exotic growth in India,*

* See a recent paper in the Journal of the Buddhist Text Society, by Pandit R. C. Shastri.

but indigenous products requiring only revival and re-invigoration,—if by divisions and unfaithfulness we do not to-day demonstrate our own ability to act together for a common end? What use is it to realise the historical background of the Gansabhawa Court of to-day, if rightly or wrongly, it is possible for any villager to feel that he can more expect justice from a foreign administrator than from one of his own people.

One of the most significant aspects of the beginnings of the movement towards unity in India has been the establishment of extra-official systems of legal arbitration. I am thinking especially of the Poona Arbitration Court. This Court, founded in 1876, consisted of leading men of the city, nearly half of them lawyers. The object was to arrange for the settlement of disputes by inexpensive private arbitration, so as to avoid the drain upon the people involved in costly litigation and the accompanying destruction of social good-will. A register of arbitrators was kept open to inspection, and disputing parties selected one or more of these by agreement. In this Court, in about 30 years, some 12,940 cases were disposed of. The total amounts involved exceeded 30 lacs of rupees. The cost of these proceedings amounted to about half a lac; if taken to the Law Courts, the cost would have been about 4¾ lacs. But much more important than the saving of money is the gain to the community in good feeling, confidence in the integrity of its own leaders, and general sense of unity and capacity for combination. I do not suggest the imitation of any particular feature of communal life whether new or old, or Eastern or Western; but I do say that there are surely some such ways as these in which we too might conserve amongst ourselves the remains of an earlier unity and add to it a wider and more comprehensive unity of modern growth.

We have after all many features of the old village system still with us, and I could wish that we should take much greater advantage of this fact than we are accustomed to do. It has not been always the Government at work against the old society; we too by our lack of faith in each other and lack of faith towards each other have done much to weaken the unity of national life. Let us instead take advantage of and use whatever remains to us of the old unity, and endeavour to build upon it, and not instead of it, a new and deeper unity.

ANANDA K. COOMARASWAMY.